SEVEN CLANS OF THE CHEROKEE SOCIETY

Cherokee Publications, Cherokee, NC 28719

First Edition
Printed in the United States of America

ISBN 978-0-935741-17-9

Illustrations by William Taylor
Design by J. Ed Sharpe

First Printing - 1993 - 15,000
Second Printing - 1995 - 30,000
Third Printing - 2000 - 15,000
Fourth Printing - 2013 - 5,000

SEVEN CLANS Of The CHEROKEE Society

by

Marcelina Reed

illustrated by

William Taylor

Cherokee Publications
Cherokee, North Carolina

TAYLOR '92 ©

The Seven Cherokee Clans

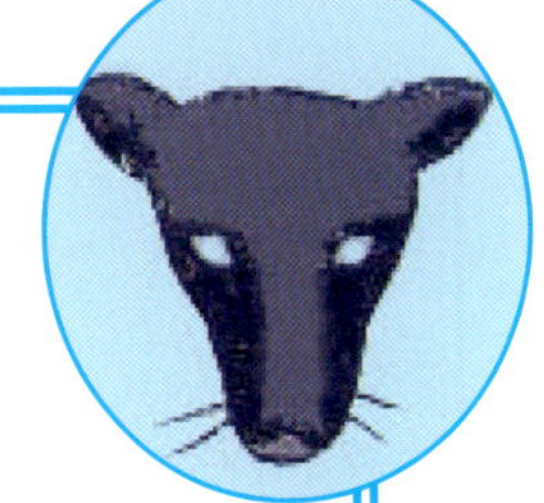

ᎠᏂ ᏌᎰᏂ *Blue or Panther* - (**A NI SA HO NI**)
They made a medicine from a bluish colored plant to keep the children well. Sometimes known also as the *Panther or Wild Cat clan.*

ᎠᏂ ᎩᎶᎯ *Long Hair* - (**A NI GI LO HI**)
also known as T*he Twister, Hair Hanging Down* or "*Wind*" clan. They wore their hair in elaborate hairdos, walked in a proud and vain manner twisting their shoulders. The Peace Chief was usually from this clan.

ᎠᏂ ᏥᏍᏆ *Bird* - (**A NI TSI S KWA**)
They were the keepers of the birds, skilled in using blowguns and snares for bird hunting. Perhaps they were messangers, as many of the birds were in the legends.

ᎠᏂ ᏬᏗ *Paint* - (**A NI WO DI**)
They made red paint and were the sorcerers and medicine men.

ᎠᏂ ᎧᏫ *Deer* - (**A NI KA WI**)
They were the keepers of the deer and were known as fast runners and deer hunters.

ᎠᏂ ᎦᏙᎨᏫ *Wild Potato* - (**A NI GA TO GE WI**)
They gathered the wild potato in swamps along streams for food. They were also known as the *Bear, Raccoon,* or *Blind Savannah* clan.

ᎠᏂ ᏩᏯ *Wolf* - (**A NI WA YAH**)
This was the largest and most prominent clan providing most of the tribe's war chiefs. They were the keepers of the wolf and the only clan who could kill a wolf.

BLUE
PANTHER

SEVEN CLANS OF THE CHEROKEE SOCIETY

From ancient times the number seven was sacred to the Cherokee. Consequently, as nomadic tribes wandering the North American continent began to settle down and take on distinctive characteristics of place, name, language and customs, it was only natural and logical that the basic arrangement of Cherokee social, religious and political life would develop into a structure of seven clans.

The seven-clan system, along with many other developments around the number seven, contributed to making the Cherokee distinctive from the many other Native American tribes. The sacred number seven permeates Cherokee legends, beliefs and customs including the seven sided council house, the sacred fire which was kindled with seven different kinds of wood , the seven directions and the seven Cherokee festivals.

The Cherokees had a matrilineal society, a social system in which their descent was traced strictly through their mother's side of the family. In the Cherokees' matrilineal kinship system a person received his mother's clan at birth and retained this clan for life, and his only kinsmen were those who could be traced through her; that is her mother's mother, mother's sisters, the children of mother's sisters and, the most important and powerful man in a child's life, the mother's brother. This social structure baffled whites.

The primary responsibility for discipline and instruction in hunting and warfare rested not with the child's father but with his maternal uncle. Not even the right of the father to stay in the home was certain because Cherokee women owned the dwellings.

+++++++++++++

If the husband was ousted from the home, he simply returned to the residence of his clan until he married again. His children, however, remained with their mother and kinsmen.

It is sometimes said that the Cherokees wore feathers of different colors to indicate their clan membership. In early literature, reference is made to a total of fourteen clans but was reduced to seven by either combining some clans or eliminating some over time.

The seven clans are frequently mentioned in the sacred formulas used by the Cherokee Indians and in some of the laws issued within the the last one hundred (100) years.

The council house was seven-sided and provided seven sections of seats within, giving each clan a section for its representatives within the governmental structure. The seven sections of seats surrounded the sacred fire.

Clan affiliation was inherited through the mother's line and marriage within this clan was strictly forbidden by law.

From the individual's perspective, four of the clans were the most important: (1) one's own clan (which was also one's mother's and maternal grandmother's), (2) one's father's clan (which was also one's paternal grandmother's),(3) maternal grandfather's clan and (4) paternal grandfather's clan.

Individuals were prohibited from marrying into the first two clans and were encouraged to marry into either the maternal grandfather's clan or paternal grandfather's clan.

+++++++++++++

As the household was the basic unit of the Cherokee social organization, residence was matrilocal (home of wife's kin group); therefore, a newly married couple lived with the wife's family.

Cherokees intermarried with whites more than with members of other Indian tribes, causing many problems with the laws of the clans. However, even though the children were of both white and Indian ancestry, they were regarded as Cherokee by their clansmen.

These intermarriages brought on many changes within the clan system, because as the Cherokees began to intermarry with the whites and blacks, the law of the clan revenge was very difficult for non-Cherokees to accept. This brought on change in the clan law which eventually merged it into the white man's court system.

+++++++++++++

In the white man's society, usually the men were in control of the land and the assets, but in the Cherokee society the women were in complete control of all property. This caused many problems with land ownership, especially when children were produced. For instance, when a Cherokee woman married a white man, he was not familiar with the law allowing the woman complete control over the land, property and children. It was difficult for him to accept the idea that if he should ever leave his wife he would be unable to take possession of property or offspring. The council dealt with this problem in 1819 by prohibiting white men from disposing of their Cherokee wive's property.

The clan provided many important functions including care for orphans and the destitute, hospitality for visiting clan members from other towns and, most important, the avenging of wrongs committed against clan members.

TAYLOR '93 ©
LONG HAIR

Clan membership was essential to one's existence as a human being within a Cherokee society because of the protection of the kinship system. Since clans were divided into white or peace clans and red or war clans, a Cherokee's clan determined a person's political alignment and his role in society. Kinship, through the law of the clans, governed social relationships, dictated possible marriage partners, designated friends, designated enemies, and regulated behavior through the system such as which kinsmen had to be respected and with which kinsmen one could be intimate.

Since kinship was matrilineal, Cherokee women probably decided the matter of adoption and often had the power to determine the fate of captives. Clans were not obligated to adopt captives; however, captives were less likely to leave the Cherokees once they were adopted into a particular clan. Captives not adopted into the clan system were, if not killed, made to be of slave status.

The slave(atsi-nahsa-i)was considered an "anomaly", that is defined as a physical human but not able to live as human because of no clanship. Rather than banish or kill them, the Cherokees supported them, recognizing that people did exist outside their kinship system. These captives functioned as deviants in the Cherokee society. The clan which adopted a captive became liable for his misdeeds as well as responsible for avenging wrongs done to him. To be without a clan in Cherokee society was to be without rights, even the right to live. A captive who was not adopted faced a distressing and unpredictable future.

The Seven Clans were groups in which each kept his clan membership for life; some were closely related and others more distantly related. Since clan membership was determined at birth, it was only natural that the child belonged to the clan of the mother since she was certain of her birth child whereas the identity of the father might, in some cases, be less certain.

B
I
R
D

If a member of a clan needed help in any manner, his clan would take care of him, and if a clan member was injured or killed by a member of another clan, his clan was responsible for revenge. No such thing as a feud would evolve, because it was understood among all clans that revenge would be taken in the event of injury or death, and the recipient clan of the revenge usually considered it justified. The type of revenge permitted could be determined by the clansmen who were selected to carry it out. There were often times when the clan of the offender would perform the revenge on a selected member of their clan to eliminate the possibility of an innocent sufferer.

All crimes such as theft of religious objects, assault on a priest, arson, treason, witchcraft, homicide, incest, stealing from the dead and intermarrying within a clan were all punishable by death.

The blood revenge was usually performed by an older male of the victim's clan if it could not be taken by his oldest brother. It was considered a disgrace if revenge was not taken. The Cherokees believed that revenge must be taken in order to free the soul of the victim and to let it pass from this world to the next.

It was the practice to avenge the victim by taking the life of the murderer himself; however, a close relative of the murderer would satisfy the revenge.

When a clan member was visiting other nearby or distant towns, he was still considered family, and the law of blood revenge held true in any location. The clans were considered close family, and they were the ideal unit for revenge since they considered themselves related as brothers and sisters.

+++++++++++++

The Ancient Law of blood revenge was abolished by the Cherokee National Government on September 11, 1808. This act of abolishment was seen to have advanced the Cherokees in civilization, and it was universally accepted by all tribes.

September 11, 1808 in Council Broom's Town

Be it known, That this day, the various clans or tribes which compose the Cherokee Nation, have unanimously passed an act of oblivion for all lives for which they may have been indebted, one to the other, and have mutually agreed that after this evening the aforesaid act shall become binding upon every clan or tribe, and the aforesaid clans or tribes, have also agreed that if, in future, any life should be lost without malice intended, the innocent aggressor shall not be accounted guilty.

*Be it known,also,*That should it happen that a brother, forgetting his natural affections, should raise his hands in anger and kill his brother, he shall be accounted guilty of murder and suffer accordingly, and if a man has a horse stolen, and overtakes the thief, and should his anger be so great as to cause him to kill him, let his blood remain on his own conscience, but no satisfaction shall be demanded for his life from his relatives or the clan he may belong to.

By order of the Seven Clans

Each village of the Cherokees had two governmental units comprised of a white and a red government. During times of peace the white government had complete control of all affairs dealing with the village. This government consisted of older and wiser men who would not make foolish decisions. In times of war all duties fell on the red government which consisted of younger men who would do well in battle.

The white or peace government consisted of the Chief of the tribe, the Chief's right-hand man, prime counselors (one from each clan unit), a council of elders, a chief speaker, messengers and officers versed in ceremonial functions. This is the organization that made the decisions which affected the tribe during their times of peace.

+++++++++++++

The red government consisted of a Great Red War Chief, The Great War Chief's Second, seven War Counselors, a War Woman, the Chief War Speaker, Messengers, Ceremonial Officers and War Scouts. The seven war counselors were in charge of declaring war when they felt the circumstances made it necessary. The War Woman's position was to declare the fate of captives and prisoners that were taken in times of war.

The war scouts reported back to the war party so decisions could be made on directions to take.

These two governments were derived from the strong beliefs of the Cherokee and their clan system, an organization supported by all in a effort to ensure survival of the tribe.

+++++++++++++

The Cherokees' attitude toward things which strayed from a general rule can best be seen in their belief system and the way in which it categorized nature. Instead of trying to obscure or to deny the existence of those things which could not be easily classified, the Cherokees paid special attention to them. In the Cherokee society, three categories of animate things occupied the world: human beings, plants and animals. Cherokees did not ignore the human characteristics of plants and animals; they magnified them, and they became major figures in the Cherokees' myths and legends, such as the bear, snake, deer and bird.

The Cherokees did not view abnormalities as causes for fear but as subjects of profound interest, and by emphasizing the exceptions of their categories they strengthened their system of classification. Some of the clan names that are still used today have the names of animals that are used in many myths and legends.

DEER

Seven continues to be a significant and sacred number to the Cherokee people, and is still highly respected today. The chief of the Cherokee people is currently elected by the people who are from townships, many of which still carry the clan names. All of the current disputes are settled in a Tribal Court and, depending on the crime committed, are forwarded to a state or federal court system in a nearby town.

Although masks were not used anciently to identify each particular clan, one can find contemporarily carved masks depicting the seven clans. Stone pipes having seven stem holes were used in the old peace councils. Now days the seven stemed pipes are produced from stone or pottery.

Marriage within a clan or to a near relative is still forbidden, a rule that continues to be enforced by many of the Cherokees.

+++++++++++++

The dramatic decline in clan affiliation occurred during the middle of the 20th Century (1940-1969). Today on the Qualla Boundary of Western North Carolina there are still a few Cherokees who can identify their clan because it has been handed down through the generations. If the clan affiliation is not known, it is very rare that it will be identified. The task is made very difficult because there was no record of clan membership kept on file.

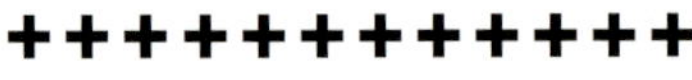

+++++++++++++

WILD
POTATO

SEVEN FESTIVALS OF THE CHEROKEE

Another example of the use of "SEVEN" in Cherokee Society was the Seven Festivals of the Cherokee always held during a new moon:

First New Moon of Spring (When the grass begins to grow)	March/April
New Green Corn Ceremony (Selutsunigististi) (When the corn was first fit to eat)	August
Ripe Corn Ceremony (Donagohuni) (Mature or ripe green corn)	September
Great New Moon Ceremony (Nuwatiegwa) (First new moon of Autumn-Cherokee New Year)	Sept./Oct.
Reconciliation & Friends-Made Ceremony (Atohuna) (Ten days after last ceremony ended)	Oct./Nov.
Bouncing Bush Feast (Elawatalegi) (Time determined at first new moon of Autumn)	Varied
The Uku Dance (Peace Chief's Dance) (Replaced the Great New Moon Ceremony for that year. Peace Chief wore all yellow and reconsecrated himself as chief.)	Every 7th Year

W O L F

Illustrations

Suggested Reading

Strickland, Rennard. Fire and the Spirits, From Clan to Court

Perdue, Theda. Slavery and the Evolution of Cherokee Society

Sharpe, Ed. The Cherokees, Past and Present

King, Duane. The Cherokee Heritage Book

Finger, John. Cherokee Americans

Mooney, James. Myths and Sacred Formulas of the Cherokee

Neely, Sharlotte. Snowbird Cherokees, People of Persistence

Lewis, Thomas M.N. & Kneberg, Madeline. Tribes That Slumber

Mails, Thomas. The Cherokee People

For more Cherokee and Native American Books

contact

CHEROKEE PUBLICATIONS
P.O. BOX 430
CHEROKEE NC 28719

Phone (800) 948-3161
Email cpubl@aol.com

Order books online:
www.Cherokeepublications.net

Birth Certificate

Sinan Antoon

شهادة ولادة

سنان أنطون

Is it a wounded bird?
Dying in the lap of a woman whose
corpse rests against the trunk of
a giant mulberry?

When its tiny wings flutter
they stain her face with blood.

Flies circle her gaping mouth.
Her eyes are staring at hell.

أهو طائر جريح؟ هذا الذي يحتضر بين ساقي امرأة،
تتّكئ جثّتها على جذع سدرة عملاقة؟

كلما رفرف جناحيه الصغيرين يرشان بقعاً صغيرة من الدم
على وجهها.

يحوم الذباب حول فمها الفاغر بينما تبحلق عيناها في الجحيم.

لكنّه يئن ويبكي مثل بني البشر.

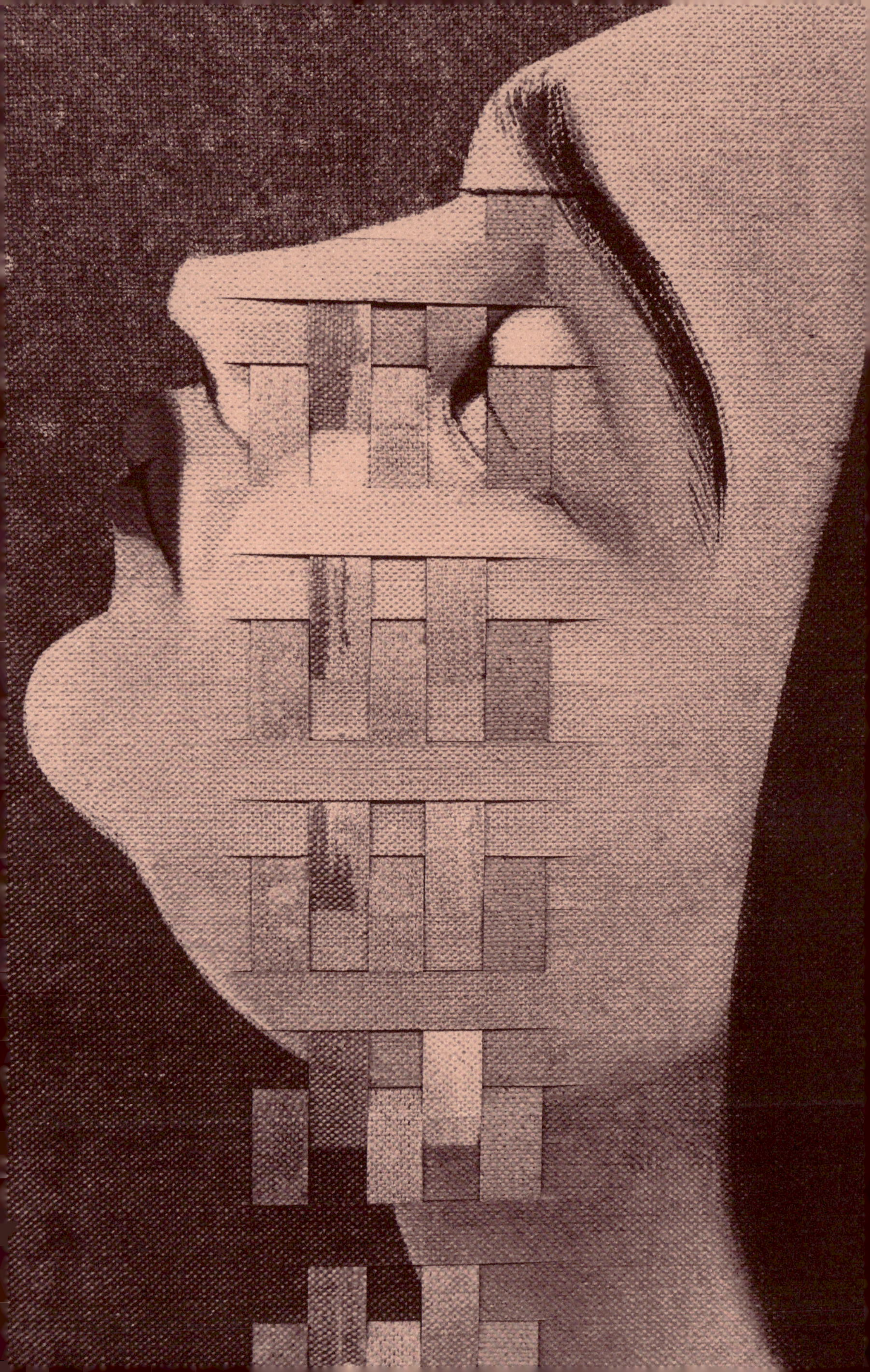

But it wails like a human.

No,
it isn't a bird.
It's a cherub covered with blood.

It was startled when it saw me
and tried to hide.

لكنّه يئن ويبكي مثل بني البشر.

كلا، ليس طائراً، بل ملاكاً
صغيراً بجناحين.

كما في لوحات العصور الوسطى.

لكنّه ملطّخ بالدم! جفل حين رآني وحاول أن يخبّئ
وجهه بين فخذيها.

I saw a knife covered with dirt and blood.
I picked it up.
I held the cherub by its wings and
raised it.

It shivered like the branches
above.

I severed its umbilical cord.
A cry soared.

I decided to rid it of its wings.

I cut them whispering:
"The sky is no more safe than the earth."

لمحت سكيناً ملوثة بالتراب والدم قرب قدمها اليمنى .
اقتربت والتقطتها .

I saw a knife covered with dirt and blood.
I picked it up.
I held the cherub by its wings and
raised it.

It shivered like the branches
above.

أمسكت بالملاك من جناحيه ورفعته . كان يرتعش مثل
أغصان السدرة

I severed its umbilical cord.
A cry soared.

قطعت الحبل السرّي الذي يربطه بأمّه . طار .
صراخه إلى السماء
قررت أن أخلّصه من جناحيه أيضاً فقصصتهما

I decided to rid it of its wings.

I cut them whispering:
"The sky is no more safe than the earth."

وأنا أردّد
"السماء ليست آمن من الأرض."

When I placed it back on the ground it crawled. . .
. . . and started looking for its first prey.

حين وضعته على الأرض أخذ يزحف . . .
بعيداً باحثاً عن فريسته الأولى .

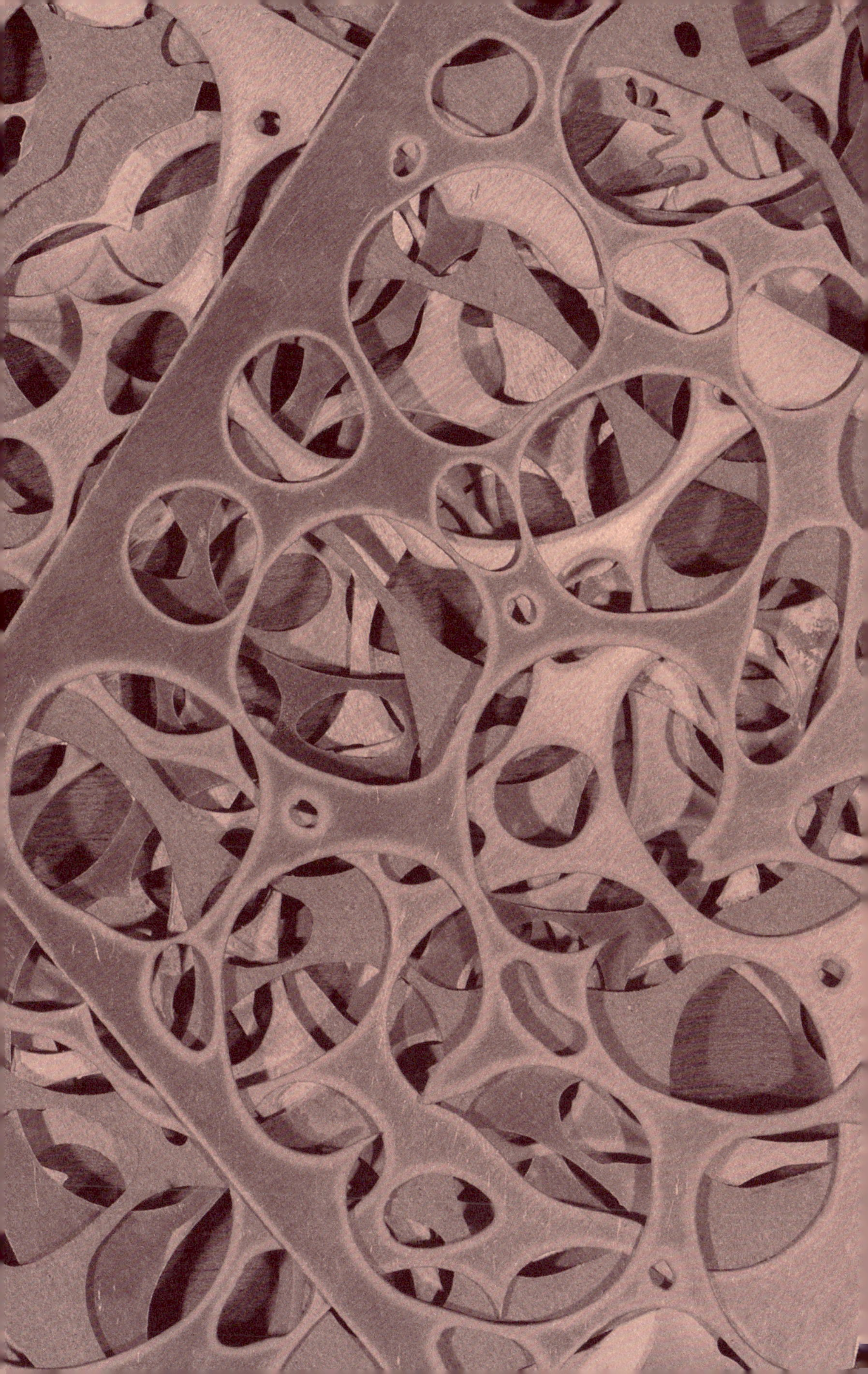

Gendering memories of Iraq—A collective performance

Hayv Kahraman

1—

Let me share with you my memories.

As my mom walked into the room she placed a medium-sized suitcase on the floor and said: it's time. She had received the instructions from our smuggler to pack one suitcase only and leave everything else behind. We packed the necessities for survival. But we also packed a *mahaffa*. The *mahaffa* is a small handheld fan, woven out of palm tree fronds. It's an emblematic symbol of Iraq and the Gulf region. But most importantly, here it was, traveling with us and our falsified passports through the Middle East, Africa, and Europe until we reached our final destination in Sweden. It now decorates our home in Sweden in what I like to call the "Iraqi corner," where several objects notoriously "Iraqi" in nature are placed and organized. This corner acts as a memorial and perhaps a shrine that carries imaginaries of a lost past. For me, the *mahaffa* has assumed a mnemonic value in which past imaginaries of "home" are both idealized and contested.

You know, when I cut my linen I almost feel like I'm doing something I'm not supposed to. Like I'm breaking the law. When I became a refugee in Sweden I moved to a small town and was a student who carefully obeyed the law—a goody two-shoes. Always having to exceed beyond my peers to prove myself worthy. After all, I was brown and so not part of their history and seen as inferior. I still have elements of this characteristic—of obeying authority at all costs. I think a lot of refugees experience this type of subordination. And when I was so engulfed and consumed by Eurocentric aesthetics (specifically that of the Renaissance), the linen, that substrate, assumed an authority of sorts. There were rules to be followed. And when I started dismantling my substrate, I felt like I was being a lawless subject. I was embarking to work on a torn surface that was the art conservator's nightmare. I had broken the law. Now what?

In that very submission, I felt a need to repair. Quickly I found another painting, I detached it from its constraining bars and started to cut strips that I then wove into the original surface. The process was palimpsestic in nature yet you could still see and feel its original layer. It wasn't restored to its original state. It was transformed. The painting, the figure, her body had traces of scars, defaced through her skin. And then another material containing another shredded body is interlaced like a weave. A synthesis of transversed bodies each with their own mnemonic itineraries. The painting, the body in the painting is the carrier. Wounded and healed and transcended. Not forgotten.

And so I get a sense of ending as I send my "lost paintings" to the garment district in LA to be shredded. Nobody at this point has seen that work except myself and the shredder. And when I receive it in fragments I am in awe of its beauty. Yards and yards of shredded lost paintings in my studio that are waiting to be reconfigured. Now each strip carries its own history. And when they are woven into the new surface there is a sense of resolution. They found their place imbedded into another.

Braiding, sewing, entwining, knitting, and inducing. Interlacing the strips of linen into her flesh. Cutting her skin in perfect lines and then mending it. The act of weaving becomes an act of mending.

Pick up the shreds. Examine and play with them.

For me the question remains: what does it mean to suture fragments in the effort to archive them and why is this so important? Maybe it comes with the territory of being a refugee, an endless activity of collecting pieces and repetitively weaving them both as a form of mourning trauma but also as a negation to erasure. Yes, I think that's my fear: that erasure. In a way I am working against that erasure in a constant effort to remember. And when I remember there is a form of repair that happens. A working through of something.

2—

Let me share with you my memories.

Running, I remember running as fast as I could and at the corner of my eyes I could see others running. This was one of those moments when time slowed down as if suspended in space. Would this moment ever end? Will I ever reach the house? The loud noise blurred the voices and screams to the point where it felt like I was running in thick fog but everything was crystal clear. The source of the siren must've been close. I was 9 at the time playing outside in a bazaar before it hit. Some people scattered inside scrambling to take shelter and some just started running. The score of this symphony was simple and repetitive, an undulating warning for an event that might or might not end our lives.

This sonic memory is different from other memories I have. It sits somewhere else in my memory bank. It encapsulates a multiple sensory perceptive that culminates in what I would call my entire experience of the war. It's the sound of "Operation

Desert Storm." And as I sat in my studio it wasn't too long into my research where I was reunited with it again. The Thunderbolt 7000 siren made by Federal Signal Corporation in Illinois and installed all around Iraq. I played this mp3 sound on my computer speakers in my studio and I was instantly transferred in time.

In his book, *Listening to War: Sound, Music, Trauma, and Survival in Wartime Iraq,* Martin Daughtry describes an interview with a mother shielding her children from the violent sounds of war by holding them tight and pressing her arms against their ears. Her body, her flesh then acts as a perfect, natural microenvironment to protect her children.

I wanted to mimic this concept of "flesh as defense" so I introduced pyramid acoustic foam in the paintings. These sound absorbers function by scattering the sound waves in several directions causing them to dissipate. An object that "detains" sound.

I started surgically cutting my linen and pushing the foam through it from the back. As it was penetrating the surface that I so meticulously prepared, I felt as if I was conducting an operation of resistance. These calculated cuts and wounds were enabling the painting to breathe, letting air pulsate through the surface from the front to the back and to the front again. Inhaling and exhaling it was reacting, resisting, defending, and accepting these sonic wounds. They're not just paintings hanging on the wall, they're hybrid shields that absorb sound and will alter that dynamic in the space they're hung.

Everyone to inhale and exhale noticeably.

The various "performances" of these female bodies, in a way assume multiple personas, which enable me to *become* someone else. Am I *betraying* myself by posing in these positions taken from the American military cards of Iraqi insurgents holding AK-47's? It was uncomfortable to use my body to mimic these pictograms yet somehow it felt natural. That sense of submission and assimilation; I am now one of you or rather *I am who you want me to be.* A violent Arab. I face the fetish of my otherness every day.

3—

Let me share with you my memories.

I remember once when my dad was driving in downtown Baghdad and we passed a narrow street that led into a larger square. I was in the front seat of the car and pointed up toward the demolished building and asked him, "What happened?"

There was a foggy air around this once-tall building—now half its size—that made me recall the many dust storms that occupied the city every now and then. "It is because of the Iran-Iraq War," he said with a low voice, as we turned the corner. That was the first time I had seen destruction of that magnitude.

I remember clinging to my mother in the basement of my uncle's house in Suleymania in northern Iraq. I remember my relatives curled around candles, waiting for the loud noises outside to stop. Despite my fear, a sense of solidarity prevailed: I was surrounded by my family, and somehow I felt protected as we all sang and played games in the dark.

When the noises stopped, I went out to play with my friends in the hopes of collecting the most bullet shells or the biggest bullet shell to impress my peers. Somewhat golden in color and quite beautiful, I remember thinking. Then suddenly the loud siren went off. It was so loud that you had to cover your ears and run. These howling sounds shook me to the very core, yet they were part of my childhood. Now they serve as a memory that both jolts me to the ground and reminds me of my vulnerable past. A past that I cherish, because I lost it. I left my life behind. The house my father built, my friends, my school, my toys.

A few years ago we sold my childhood home in Baghdad. This was difficult. I attributed that home to a tangible space, a space that encapsulated memories I did not want to lose. My childhood memories were interrupted because of war. My history was carved into those walls not only intimately but literally so. Growing up, I used the four walls of an entire room as my canvas and filled them with characters, narratives, concerns, jokes, and discoveries. When our home sold, a part of me faded. We tried to hold on to it as long as we could, but my father has two daughters, and we couldn't have inherited the house. The laws in Iraq prohibit a female member of the family from inheriting a property, so our home would have had to go to the next closest male kin. Of course, there was the matter that we might return, but this was always dismissed by my family and me partly because of the political situation, but also because of the growing dissociation with our home.

I needed to paint a record of these homes, some still standing, some not. The act of tracing these lines on the panels makes me feel that I'm archiving and preserving a history somehow. Every line I paint corresponds to a tangible structure, a wall, a door, a room that was once inhabited and had a narrative in its own right. It might even still be there. I also sometimes imagine myself as an archaeologist, digging and tracing these lines to research and recover a past and perhaps a connection with it.

The figures are all extensions of my own body, as I photograph myself and use these images to produce the figures. They are repeated over and over again in the work as a form of assertion and affirmation. They are painted transparently on the brown panels, resembling ghosts that are neither here nor there. You see, as an immigrant or refugee, I found that the best method to survive is to imitate, and maybe I did it too well, as I sometimes feel like I'm flickering in and out of multiple worlds. When I visit Sweden I always get an out-of-body experience. It is like I can see myself walking the streets, being watched, being judged for the color of my skin. I'm automatically degraded to a second-class citizen. A refugee: an *invandrare*. With that also comes a sense of erasure and a peculiar sense of being a nobody yet being hyper visible via my skin. And so in this oscillating state of being and disappearance, *She* roams the substrate in a spectral dance. Shifting between absence and solidity.

Everyone to imitate her body gesture.

4—

Let me share with you my memories.

I remember that it was pitch black outside, and our car was finally packed. As we drove away, I could see my grandmother in the back window tossing water from a glass behind the car for good luck. As if that small glass of water would purify our journey through the night. My grandmother's water was a promise of return to the motherland. I never returned.

We had hired a smuggler to take us to a faraway land where it was safe. I remember that when we reached Stockholm Arlanda—the airport in Sweden—my mom took my sister and me to the bathroom, ripped our Iraqi passports into small shreds, and flushed them down the toilet. The bits and pieces floated on the surface of the rippled water for a few seconds before sinking in and then disappearing quickly in a whirl. "Follow me," she said, as she walked us to the immigration desk. It was around 3:30 in the afternoon, and my sister and I had to wait outside in the playroom while my mother talked to the police. I looked outside through the window, and it was pitch black again.

Everyone to get up follow her to walk in front of the painting *Target* then go back to sit down.

Here I started my new life as a war refugee, marked by my black hair and brown skin among the tall blond kids in my class. This is my identity, and it will always be my identity. I had to learn the tricks of the trade. I was this peculiar creature walking in the desert snow of Sweden, but when they spoke to me, they became assured and comforted, because I made it a point to master their tongue. At least phonetically, I could cover myself and be in disguise. If you spoke to me on the phone you would've thought that you had spoken to a native Swede! Yes, I did assimilate, I did adapt, and I did try my best to imitate them. Maybe they would see me as one of them if I acted more like them and forgot my old self. And I did forget for a while. But not much later I realized that bleaching my skin, my hair, and my tongue was not of any help. No matter how hard I tried to erase myself, I would always be the other person who carried her native home on her back. I will always be the refugee.

You know, I attended the music and ballet school in central Baghdad. Dance (specifically ballet) was one of my dreams when I was growing up. I wanted to become a ballerina. I was even chosen to be one of the Four Swans in Swan Lake. And in the midst of our comprehensive rehearsals the war started and my role—that I was so proud to have received—was given to someone else because I was set to flee Iraq. When I settled in Sweden, I enrolled in ballet classes but decided to leave. My teacher made it clear that Black Swans were not welcome in Tchaikovsky's lake. I could do my Arabian *saut de chameau*, but *le saut de biche* was not made for the likes of me, i.e. the daughters of Othello, the Moor.

Everyone to flip their papers with her.

When I was pregnant, this yearning to connect with my Iraqi self grew even stronger. I started wanting and needing my daughter to know where her mother was from.

And so, as I was flipping through a children's book at the store a few weeks after finding out that I was pregnant, I remembered *Maqamat al-Hariri's* collection of short stories. These are 13th-century illuminated manuscripts made by the Baghdad school of miniature painting describing the everyday life of Iraqis at the time. What a perfect way to describe my past life in Iraq to my daughter, I thought! So the *maqamat* served as formal and conceptual frameworks behind ideas of what it means to be an Iraqi today, or rather, an Iraqi immigrant and refugee. It also became a way for me to record my own dissociation with my culture and perhaps a yearning to reconnect with it.

The element of language and connecting to the written Arabic word was vital in these works. I was actively relearning how to write. I didn't want to copy blindly. I took my time to examine the original text, each letter, the thickness of the stroke, the shape, the angle. But I was determined not to force anything. I wanted it to be as natural as possible. I was *re-learning* how to write my language and read and speak my mother tongue. The tongue that I don't use anymore and have grown to forget. The tongue I regret not having continued to learn.

I look at these Arabic letters with estranged eyes now. I was exported and so was my language. But it's also my fault for not having kept it alive. I was too busy learning the western tongue and training my eyes to adapt to English letters. I can now see these Arabic letters from the perspective of an American or a Swede and that terrifies me. It makes me want to reiterate them, paint them, write them, re-learn them, and re-memorize them; perhaps recover them. I am on the search for recapturing my amputated mother tongue. I am searching for my 9-year-old self who spoke and wrote fluent Arabic. My biggest fear is that if I were to return one day, neither my grandmother's water nor the earth it irrigated for good luck would ever recognize me.

5—

She walks around the table.

Let me share with you my memories.
I remember looking outside the car window and seeing a mirage and thinking how similar this country is to mine. Yet here I was, riddled with guilt and frustration about buying my groceries at Target.

I was set to move again but this time farther away, to a country that is at war with my own. To a country that I never thought I'd set foot in, even though I spoke its language and felt somewhat familiar with its culture. You see, growing up in Baghdad, I attended an international/American school, so English and Arabic were equally integrated into my vocabulary. When I fled to Sweden after the first Gulf War, the American media was already ingrained in the culture. It was as if I were being followed. From Iraq to Sweden to Italy and now to the United States. But this was different. This time something happened in my identity as a woman. One day I started drawing a figure. I played around with the figure, and slowly *She* started emerging. It was all very natural, as if I've known her for a while. As if she had always been there but had never surfaced. That day she finally did. She gave me a voice to speak about her. She told me that she was hung in the name of honor. I didn't understand. What did she mean? Her brother interjected and said she was raped and became pregnant. She has brought shame to our family and my father, and I had to restore and protect that honor.

But that's not all. She'd rather pour kerosene on her body, pick up a match that she normally uses for cooking, and ignite herself. These are women just like you and me. At the time I was one of them, but I didn't know that I was. It was easier to speak about *her* than to look at my own life. Yes, I was asleep and deeply so. But they, these figures, these women paved an outlet that my deepest self needed to uncover. I needed a change. A violent change. I wanted to shed my skin and toss it in the trash and never look back again in the hopes that a new skin would eventually grow. I wanted to constrain it. To confine it. To restrict it to this rectangle. After all, that's what I was used to. I was a worn body being beat to the ground.

It's a crude act, this detaching of a limb. The shape of each slice is derived from the digital, three-dimensional scan of my body that was then cross-sectioned into quarter-inch horizontal slices.

I needed to extract my body: to dismantle it and to fragment it. It was the only way to wake myself up. As I stood there, my nude body being photographed by a man operating this scanning device, I felt a loss of agency. A resignation and submission that made me somehow feel domesticated, comfortable, and . . . familiar.

One woman strokes another beside her.

The results of looking at my body through a computer screen were cathartic. *She* became a surface to dissect and divide and analyze. The violent and nonchalant aspect of plane-sectioning a body speaks to a similar detachment and separation that occurs in diasporic peoples. But it was also something I needed to do as a woman. The depiction of these cross-sections eliminated the "social" in the body for me and reduced it to mere function: object and flesh. It erased the embodied sociocultural experiences that I feel are contingent on our perceptions and views of the world. And so I needed to cleanse my body with water and scrub it down. I needed to erase my old body, and I needed to restore and rebuild it after waking up. Never will I let myself sleep as my brown skin grows back again.

Am I a commodity? Are my paintings and figures a commodity? I pose in the nude and photograph my body to use as outlines for paintings. My figures then are visual transitions of my own body. The figures are rendered to fit the occidental pleasures. White flesh. Transparent flesh. Posing in compositions directly taken from the Renaissance. Conforming to what *they* think is ideal. Neglecting everything else. Colonizing my own body to then be displayed gracefully in my rectangular panels. Carnal and visceral palpability. I provide for you in my rectangles. I know you like it. That's why I paint it. To catch your gaze. To activate your gaze. I want you to buy me so you can look at me all day long. I'm your little oriental pussycat. You can pet me if you like.

Exhibition Checklist

Barricade 1, 2018
Oil on linen
50 × 78 in.
Courtesy of the artist and
Susanne Vielmetter
Los Angeles Projects

Barricade 2, 2018
Oil on linen
70 × 40 in.
Pomona College Collection.
Museum purchase made with
funds provided by The Frederick
Hammersley Foundation and the
Dr. Louise M. Paris Fund

Clock, 2017
Oil, linen, RSG, and
pigment on paper
25 × 22¾ in.
Courtesy of the artist and
Susanne Vielmetter
Los Angeles Projects

Read me from right to left, 2017
Oil on linen triptych
78 × 150 in.
WASSART Collection,
Switzerland

Star, 2017
Oil, linen, RSG, and
pigment on paper
25 × 22¾ in.
Courtesy of the artist and
Susanne Vielmetter
Los Angeles Projects

Acknowledgments

"Hayv Kahraman" is the fifty-second exhibition in the Pomona College Museum of Art's Project Series. The Museum's Project Series, an ongoing program of focused exhibitions of work by Southern California artists, has always relied on the generous support of many individuals and groups, in particular longtime supporters the Pasadena Art Alliance. It has been a privilege to work with patrons who so strongly believe in artists and their work.

I extend deep gratitude to Hayv Kahraman for this opportunity to present her work in the exhibition, publication, and performance at Pomona College. This exhibition would not have happened without former curatorial assistant Noor Asif, who brought Kahraman's paintings to my attention in 2016. For support of the exhibition and publication, many thanks are due to Susanne Vielmetter and Ariel Pittman at Susanne Vielmetter Los Angeles Projects; Elisabeth Sann at Jack Shainman Gallery in New York; and Sunny Rahbar and Marina Iordan at The Third Line in Dubai. This book is greatly enhanced by the texts from Madina Tlostanova and Sinan Antoon. I am indebted to designer Kimberly Varella for her vision and patience. Curatorial assistant Nidhi Gandhi ably copy-edited the publication and provided invaluable assistance.

I am grateful to my colleagues at the Pomona College Museum of Art: Kathleen Howe, Justine Bae, Barbara Ditlinger, Steve Comba, jill moniz, Gary Murphy, and David Hendren for their support throughout the planning and presentation of this project.

— Rebecca McGrew
Senior Curator
Pomona College Museum of Art

Contributor's Biographies

Hayv Kahraman was born in Baghdad, Iraq in 1981, and now lives and works in Los Angeles. Kahraman's recent solo exhibitions include "Acts of Reparation," Contemporary Art Museum St. Louis, St. Louis, Missouri (2017); "Hayv Kahraman," Joslyn Museum of Art, Omaha, Nebraska (2016); "Sound Wounds," Asian Art Museum, San Francisco (2016); "Gendering memories of Iraq—A collective performance," which has been staged at Contemporary Art Museum St. Louis (2017), Birmingham Museum of Art, Birmingham, Alabama (2016), Nelson-Atkins Museum of Art, Kansas City, Missouri (2014), and Duke University, Durham, North Carolina (2014); "Reweaving Migrant Inscriptions," Jack Shainman Gallery, New York (2016); "Audible Inaudible," The Third Line, Dubai, United Arab Emirates (2016); and "How Iraqi are you?," Jack Shainman Gallery (2015). Recent group exhibitions include: "Dreamers Awake," White Cube, London (2017); "The Centre Cannot Hold," Near East, Istanbul (2017); "No Man's Land: Women Artists from the Rubell Family Collection," National Museum of Women in the Arts, Miami (2016); "UNREALISM: Presented by Larry Gagosian and Jeffrey Deitch," Miami Design District, Miami (2015); and "June: A Painting Show," Sadie Coles HQ, London (2015). Kahraman was shortlisted for the 2018 and the 2011 Jameel Prize at the Victoria and Albert Museum and has received the "Excellence in Cultural Creativity" award from the Global Thinkers Forum.

Sinan Antoon is a poet, novelist, translator, and scholar. He is an Associate Professor at New York University's Gallatin School and co-founder and co-editor of *Jadaliyya*. His most recent publications include *Laylun Wahidun fi Kull al-Mudun* (Dar al-Jamal, 2010), *Ya Maryam* (Dar al-Jamal, 2012, 2013), *Wahdaha Shajarat al-Rumman* (translated as *The Corpse Washer*, Yale University Press, 2013), *The Poetics of the Obscene: Ibn al-Hajjaj and Sukhf* (Palgrave Macmillan, 2013), and *Fihris* (Dar al-Jamal, 2016). His poems and essays in Arabic have appeared in *as-Safir, al-Adab, al-Akhbar, Bidayat, al-Hayat, Majallat al-Dirasat al-Filastiniyya, Masharef* and in English in *The Nation, Middle East Report, Al-Ahram Weekly, Banipal, Journal of Palestine Studies, The Massachusetts Review, World Literature Today, Ploughshares, Washington Square Journal*, and *The New York Times*.

Rebecca McGrew is senior curator at the Pomona College Museum of Art. Recent exhibitions include "Prometheus 2017: Four Artists from Mexico Revisit Orozco" (2017) as part of the Getty Foundation's Pacific Standard Time: LA/LA initiative, "R.S.V.P. Los Angeles: The Project Series at Pomona" (2015), "Project Series 51: Incendiary Traces" (2017), "Project Series 50: Brenna Youngblood" (2015), "Andrea Bowers: #sweetjane" (2014), and "Project Series 49: Sam Falls, Ferns and Palms" (2014). She has organized many other exhibitions, including the award-winning and critically acclaimed "It Happened at Pomona: Art at the Edge of Los Angeles 1969–1973" (co-organized with Glenn Phillips, 2011–12), "Steve Roden: when words become forms" (2010), "Hunches, Geometrics, Organics: Paintings by Frederick Hammersley" (2007), "Ed Ruscha/ Raymond Pettibon: The Holy Bible and THE END" (2006), and "The 21st Century Odyssey Part II: The Performances of Barbara T. Smith" (2005). McGrew is the recipient of a Getty Curatorial Research Fellowship (2007) and Getty Foundation grants under the Pacific Standard Time initiatives in 2009–11 and 2014–15.

Madina Tlostanova is a decolonial thinker, writer, and professor of postcolonial feminisms at Linköping University (Sweden). She focuses on decolonial thought, non-Western feminism, postsocialist studies, and contemporary art. Her most recent books include *Learning to Unlearn: Decolonial Reflections from Eurasia and the Americas*, co-authored with Walter Mignolo (Ohio State University Press, 2012), *Postcolonialism and Postsocialism in Fiction and Art: Resistance and Re-existence* (Palgrave, 2017), and the forthcoming *What Does It Mean to Be Post-Soviet? Decolonial Art from the Ruins of the Soviet Empire* (Duke University Press, 2018).

This catalog was published on the occasion of the exhibition "Project Series 52: Hayv Kahraman," presented at the Pomona College Museum of Art, September 4–December 22, 2018.

This publication is supported in part by the Pasadena Arts Alliance, Pasadena, CA. Additional support provided by Susanne Vielmetter Los Angeles Projects, Los Angeles; Jack Shainman Gallery, New York; and The Third Line, Dubai, United Arab Emirates.

POMONA COLLEGE
MUSEUM OF ART

Pomona College Museum of Art
333 North College Way
Claremont, CA 91711
www.pomona.edu/museum
1-909-621-8283

ISBN 978-0-9979306-2-7

Available through D.A.P./
Distributed Art Publishers, Inc.
155 Sixth Avenue
New York, NY 10013
www.artbook.com

Copy Editing:
Nidhi Gandhi
Rebecca McGrew

Design:
Kimberly Varella,
Content Object Design Studio

Color Separations:
Echelon Color, Santa Monica, California

Printing and Binding:
Conti Tipocolor, Italy

Credits:
Cover, back cover: Courtesy of the artist; pp. 1–3, 8–15, 23–27, 30–32, 70: © Hayv Kahraman, courtesy of the artist and Jack Shainman Gallery, New York; pp. 5–6, 16–18: Courtesy of the artist and Susanne Vielmetter Los Angeles Projects, Los Angeles, photography: Ian Byers-Gamber; pp. 19–21: Courtesy of the artist and Susanne Vielmetter Los Angeles Projects, Los Angeles, photography: Jason Findley; pp. 28–29: © Hayv Kahraman, courtesy of the artist and Third Line Gallery, Dubai; pp. 53–69, 75–96: photography; Ian Byers-Gamber.

On the cover and back cover:
Process photograph of dyeing technique from Hayv Kahraman's studio, 2017.

Pages 53–69, 75–96:
Photographs from Hayv Kahraman's studio, 2018.

Page 70:
Detail of *Mnemonic Artifact 1*, 2017.
Oil on linen, 70 × 54 in.

Lighter
Darker
Destruction
Ambush
Target Type
Location of Attacker
Traffic Stop
Concealed weapons
Lesions
Bleeding
How long has animal been sick?
IED CONCEALMENT
AMBUSH
Where is the bomb?

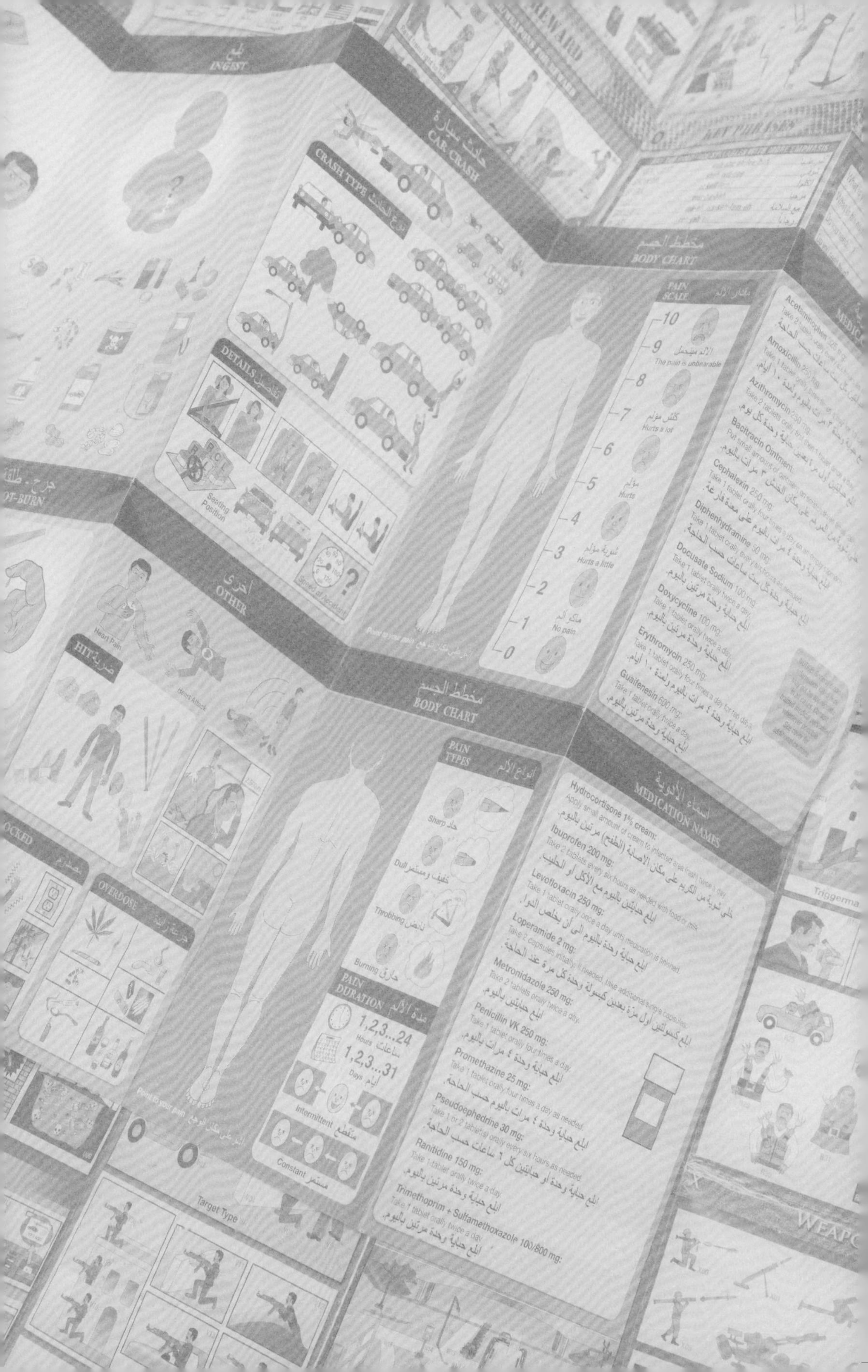

INGEST
حادث سيارة
CAR CRASH
CRASH TYPE نوع الحادث
DETAILS تفاصيل
Seating Position
Speed of Accident
?
أخرى
OTHER
Heart Pain
Heart Attack
HIT ضربة
OVERDOSE
مخطط الجسم
BODY CHART
PAIN SCALE مقدار الألم
10
9 الألم متحمل
The pain is unbearable
8
7 كلش مؤلم
Hurts a lot
6
5 مؤلم
Hurts
4
3 شوية مؤلم
Hurts a little
2
1 ماكو ألم
No pain
0
Point to your pain
مخطط الجسم
BODY CHART
PAIN TYPES أنواع الألم
Sharp حاد
Dull خفيف ومستمر
Throbbing نابض
Burning حارق
PAIN DURATION مدة الألم
1,2,3...24
Hours ساعات
1,2,3...31
Days أيام
Intermittent متقطع
Constant مستمر
Point to your pain
Target Type
KEY PHRASES
REWARD
Acetaminophen 325 mg:
Amoxicillin 250 mg:
Take 1 tablet orally three times a day for 10 days.
Azithromycin 250 mg:
Take 2 tablets orally first then 1 tablet once a day.
Bacitracin Ointment:
Cephalexin 250 mg:
Take 1 tablet orally four times a day on an empty stomach.
Diphenhydramine 50 mg:
Take 1 tablet orally every six hours as needed.
Docusate Sodium 100 mg:
Take 1 tablet orally twice a day.
Doxycycline 100 mg:
Take 1 tablet orally twice a day.
Erythromycin 250 mg:
Take 1 tablet orally four times a day for ten days.
Guaifenesin 600 mg:
Take 1 tablet orally twice a day.
أسماء الأدوية
MEDICATION NAMES
Hydrocortisone 1% cream:
Apply small amount of cream to infected area (rash) twice a day.
Ibuprofen 200 mg:
Take 2 tablets every six hours as needed with food or milk.
Levofloxacin 250 mg:
Take 1 tablet orally once a day until medication is finished.
Loperamide 2 mg:
Take 2 capsules initially. If needed, take additional single capsules.
Metronidazole 250 mg:
Take 2 tablets orally twice a day.
Penicillin VK 250 mg:
Take 1 tablet orally four times a day.
Promethazine 25 mg:
Take 1 tablet orally four times a day as needed.
Pseudoephedrine 30 mg:
Take 1 or 2 tablet(s) orally every six hours as needed.
Ranitidine 150 mg:
Take 1 tablet orally twice a day.
Trimethoprim + Sulfamethoxazole 100/800 mg:
Take 1 tablet orally twice a day.
Triggerma
WEAPO